Discovering
FOXES

Miranda MacQuitty

Discovering Nature

Discovering Ants
Discovering Bees and Wasps
Discovering Beetles
Discovering Birds of Prey
Discovering Butterflies and Moths
Discovering Crabs and Lobsters
Discovering Crickets and Grasshoppers
Discovering Damselflies and Dragonflies
Discovering Deer
Discovering Ducks and Geese
Discovering Flies
Discovering Flowering Plants

Discovering Foxes
Discovering Freshwater Fish
Discovering Frogs and Toads
Discovering Fungi
Discovering Hedgehogs
Discovering Rabbits and Hares
Discovering Rats and Mice
Discovering Saltwater Fish
Discovering Sea Birds
Discovering Slugs and Snails
Discovering Snakes and Lizards
Discovering Spiders
Discovering Squirrels
Discovering Worms

Further titles are in preparation

Editor: Clare Chandler

All photographs from Oxford Scientific Films

First published in 1988 by
Wayland (Publishers) Limited
61 Western Road, Hove
East Sussex BN3 1JD, England

British Library Cataloguing in Publication Data
MacQuitty, Miranda
    Discovering foxes.—(Discovering nature).
    1. Foxes—Juvenile literature
    I. Title   II. Series
    599.74′442   QL737.C22

ISBN 1–85210–318–3

Typeset by DP Press Limited, Sevenoaks, Kent
Printed and bound in Italy by Sagdos S.p.A., Milan

Cover
A red fox keeps a look-out from among some bushes.

Frontispiece
A red fox can run very fast.

Contents

1
Introducing Foxes

With its ears pricked up this young red fox looks very alert.

Foxes are found in many different countries around the world. They live in all sorts of places ranging from the seashore to mountains, from deserts to the icy Arctic, and from the countryside to towns. Altogether there are twenty-one different kinds of foxes. One of these, the Arctic fox, lives in the very cold north polar region. Seven other kinds of foxes are only found in South America, and the rest live in Europe, Asia and North and South America.

The fox we know best of all is the red fox which has a lovely reddish brown coat and a bushy white-tipped tail. You may have seen this kind of fox as it can be found on farmland as well as in towns and cities. Red foxes live mainly in the **northern hemisphere**. But they also thrive in Australia, where they were brought from Europe over 100 years ago, to be hunted.

In some countries, as people take over more land for farming and building towns, foxes are declining in numbers. The small-eared dog fox from South America could be under

Male foxes are called dogs and female foxes vixens. This is a dog fox.

threat because the tropical forests where it lives are being cut down.

Foxes and Their Relatives

Foxes belong to the dog family which also includes domestic dogs, jackals, wolves, coyotes, and a variety of wild dogs. All these kinds of dogs mostly eat other animals rather than plants. Such meat eaters are called

Black-backed jackals often hunt small gazelles in pairs. They are found in Africa.

carnivores. Some members of the dog family, like wolves, hunt in packs to capture large animals, such as moose, but foxes hunt alone and catch small animals, like mice and insects.

Domestic dogs are thought to be more similar to wolves than they are to foxes. The ancestors of our pet dogs may well have been orphaned wolf pups which were adopted by people thousands of years ago.

All members of the dog family have four toes on each foot. At the tip of the toe is a long claw which cannot be drawn in like cats' claws. Almost all members of the dog family have an additional small toe on the inside of the front legs above the paws.

They also have long jaws and strong teeth. There are four large sharp teeth at the front corners of the mouth. These are the canine teeth and are used to kill animals and to tear apart food. Most members of the dog family have long tails and good fur coats.

The grey wolf is larger than foxes and other members of the dog family.

What Foxes Look Like

All foxes have sharp snouts, large ears and long bushy tails. Like other members of the dog family, foxes have long legs and are good runners. Foxes are smaller than many of their relatives, especially wolves. Of all the foxes, the fennec fox is the smallest. An adult fennec fox weighs just over one kilogram. A fully grown grey wolf can be fifty times heavier than a fennec fox.

Foxes have a good coat of fur. The outer part of the coat has long hairs and beneath them are short hairs which grow close to the fox's skin. In the cooler regions of the world, foxes replace their thick winter coats with a shorter summer coat. They do this by shedding their fur which is called

The Cape fox of southern Africa has long legs and big ears.

An Arctic fox in its thick fluffy winter coat.

An Arctic fox in its dark summer coat.

moulting. Red foxes start to lose their heavy winter coat in spring and by the middle of summer have grown a new short coat. As the weather gets colder again in the autumn the red fox's coat gets thicker and longer to keep it warm in the winter.

Red foxes become slightly darker when they are moulting. Only the Arctic fox completely changes colour by moulting and growing a new coat. In winter most Arctic foxes are white. In spring they shed their white fur and grow a new brownish grey coat. In autumn Arctic foxes moult again and grow a new white coat.

2
Where Foxes Live

The small fennec fox has huge ears to help it lose heat in its hot desert home.

Deserts and Grasslands

Some foxes live in deserts and are able to tolerate very hot and dry conditions. Fennec foxes live in sandy deserts of North Africa and Arabia. They are typical desert foxes with their large ears, pale fur and furry feet.

Large ears help desert foxes to keep cool because they lose excess heat through them. The fennec fox's ears are very large in comparison to its small body. Pale coloured fur also helps desert foxes to keep cool because it absorbs less heat than dark fur. Another advantage of a pale coat is that it matches the colour of the sandy desert soil. So desert foxes are hidden from their enemies and from animals they are hunting. This sort of disguise is called **camouflage**.

Desert foxes try to keep out of the hot sun during the day by staying in their **dens**. They usually come out after dark to find food. If a fennec fox does go out in the day, its feet are protected from the burning hot ground by fur on the soles of its paws.

Other foxes such as the bat-eared fox and the Cape fox live in grasslands and generally dry regions of Africa. These places can be hot too. So bat-eared and Cape foxes also have large ears which help them keep cool. Large ears also help the bat-eared fox to detect the sounds made by small insects which it likes to eat.

A bat-eared fox in the dry grasslands of South Africa.

Arctic

The vast cold lands and ice packs around the North Pole are home to the Arctic fox. On land only small plants and shrubs survive because it is so cold. The deeper part of the soil is

In some places Arctic foxes are not afraid of people and will eat scraps of food put out for them.

frozen all through the year. This cold treeless region is called Arctic **tundra**.

Arctic foxes roam about on the ice

sheets that never melt around the North Pole and in the middle of Greenland. Those living on the shores of the Arctic Ocean will go out on to the ice that forms when the sea freezes over in winter.

The Arctic fox is well able to tolerate such cold conditions. In winter it has a very thick fur coat to keep it warm. Little of its body heat is lost through its small, furry and rounded ears. In comparison to other foxes the Arctic fox has a short **muzzle** and legs which also help it to conserve heat.

Like desert foxes, the Arctic fox has fur on the soles of its paws. Furry paws are good insulation against extreme heat or cold. This is rather like us wearing mittens to take a hot dish out of the oven or to keep our

The thick fur of an Arctic fox covers its ears and will help to keep it warm.

hands warm while making snowballs.

Arctic foxes that live in the middle of big land masses, such as Alaska and Siberia where there is a lot of snow in winter, are mostly white. White Arctic foxes are hard to see in the snow. Those foxes living on the islands and coasts of the Arctic Ocean where there is less snow cover tend to be bluish-grey in winter. This type of Arctic fox is called a blue fox.

Woods, Farmland and Cities

Some foxes prefer the dense cover of trees to open areas. The American grey fox lives in woods. It is an unusual fox because it can climb trees. To push itself up a tree, it digs the long claws on its back feet into the trunk. Climbing trees is a good way for American grey foxes to get away from their enemies, such as hunters. The American grey fox itself hunts among the branches for birds and other animals. The crab-eating fox is another fox that likes to live amongst trees. It is found in the tropical forests of South America.

Both these woodland foxes are sometimes found on farmland or on the edge of towns. The fox most often seen in towns and cities is the red fox. It lives happily in big cities like London and New York. Within towns and cities the red fox likes large gardens, railway embankments, rough ground and parks, especially if they are overgrown with brambles, bushes and weeds which give foxes somewhere to shelter.

Red foxes usually live on farmland or at the edges of woods. But during

An American grey fox is safe from its enemies high up in the branches of a tree.

the past fifty years, more and more have appeared in towns and cities. Nobody is exactly sure why these foxes set up home here. They may have moved into town because they liked the large gardens and parks. Or

Red foxes like to live in cities. Here is one near Tower Bridge in London.

we may have moved into their home when our towns and cities became larger, taking over the countryside.

3
Food for Foxes

A young fox eating a moorhen. It chews on the bird's leg with its sharp teeth.

What Foxes Like to Eat

Most foxes are not fussy about what they eat. Their diet includes a wide variety of food such as small animals like mice, voles, and insects as well as fruit. Usually foxes eat whatever they can find. This depends on where they live and the season of the year.

Red foxes living in towns and cities will eat scraps of food in garbage, along with a variety of small animals as well as fruit and vegetables. In spring, town and country red foxes find many birds to eat. In autumn fruit, like fallen apples, is a good source of food.

Crab-eating foxes eat crabs and crayfish. But like other foxes their diet is varied and includes birds, insects, rabbits, fruit and seeds. Bat-eared foxes are unusual because they mainly eat insects like termites and beetles. They find them by listening to the

Above *A city fox sniffs for food in a dustbin.*

about they will bury it in a safe place for eating later. Birds' eggs are a favourite food as they keep well stored in the ground. Foxes are able to carry eggs in their mouths and then bury them without breaking the eggs. The Arctic fox hides food during the summer to help it survive the long cold winter when food is scarce.

Below *The Cape fox likes to eat meat as well as fruit, berries and the roots of plants.*

noises these insects make. Even an insect lurking underground can be heard by a bat-eared fox which quickly digs it up with one forepaw and devours it.

Foxes generally have small appetites. If there is plenty of food

Foxes as Hunters

Foxes do not hunt in packs but go off by themselves in search of small animals. They catch mice and similar animals by leaping into the air and landing on them with their forepaws. Arctic foxes catch small mice-like animals called lemmings in this way. In winter Arctic foxes have to find the lemmings in their tunnels and nests under the snow. They listen hard for the noises made by the lemmings moving about and pounce on them through the snow.

By listening carefully foxes can find mice and other small animals hiding in long grass and bushes. To catch a mouse the fox leaps high off the ground.

Arctic foxes find plenty to eat in spring and summer. Those living inland feast on lemmings. Arctic foxes living near the seashore eat sea birds that nest on the cliffs and marine life, like crabs and fish. In winter when food is scarce some Arctic foxes follow polar bears and take scraps from the seals they kill.

A rabbit makes a good meal for a red fox.

Most foxes are **nocturnal** hunters which means they are active during the night. But Arctic foxes hunt at any time except in snow storms when they take shelter. Red foxes sometimes hunt in the day especially if they have young to feed.

4
Family Life

A vixen in her den where she will bring up her family.

Courtship and Mating

Although foxes hunt by themselves, some like to live together in small family groups. Males and females of all kinds of foxes get together once a year to **mate** and produce babies. Male foxes are called dogs and female foxes vixens. Most foxes only have one partner. Vixens can become **pregnant** just once a year. This is when they mate with dog foxes.

Vixens need a safe place or den in which to bring up their cubs. Some foxes, like the fennec fox, have permanent dens in which to live and bring up their cubs. Others, like red fox vixens, search for a den when they are pregnant. Foxes make their family home in a variety of places. Some use burrows which they either dig themselves or take over from other animals. Others hide away under rocks or in dense bushes. Red foxes in

towns will dig holes under houses and garden sheds. Foxes often return to the same den year after year. Each time they may make it a bit larger and more comfortable for their family.

Sometimes foxes will make their

Foxes fight each other during the breeding season.

dens close together. Red foxes living in towns may do this where there is a shortage of suitable places.

Caring for Their Cubs

About two months after mating a vixen will give birth to her cubs. Most foxes give birth to between one and six cubs. This is called a **litter**. Young cubs look very different from their parents. Those of the red fox have grey black fur and short rounded snouts. They are also blind and deaf when newly born. At first the mother feeds her young with her own milk. In cold climates she stays with her cubs nearly all the time to keep them warm for their first few weeks of life.

While the mother is looking after her cubs the father may bring her food. When the cubs are several weeks old she may go off to hunt herself, although she returns frequently to nurse and care for her

A very young red fox cub. See how different it looks to an adult fox.

cubs. After three or four weeks the cubs may come out of the den to explore and they begin to eat solid food. Red fox and Arctic fox parents are sometimes helped in the task of raising their cubs by their daughters from the previous year's litter.

As the cubs grow up they look more like their parents. They play with each other outside the den and learn to find food. Their parents spend less time with them. When the cubs are fully grown they move off to find new areas to live in. These areas are called **home ranges**, and they should be large enough for the fox to find enough food to survive. Some of the litter may stay in the same area although they too will move away if food is scarce. Red foxes living in towns where there is plenty of food may share their home range with another fox family.

A vixen keeps close watch over her cubs.

Fox Talk

Foxes make noises rather like pet dogs. They can whine, yelp, bark, howl and growl. Newborn cubs whine to get their mother's attention. Older cubs will yelp if they are lost. When out of the den the vixen will warn her cubs of danger by barking. Adult foxes often keep in touch with each other by barking or howling especially in the breeding season. Red foxes sometimes make a sound like a scream just to say hello to other foxes.

When foxes meet they tell each other how they are feeling by making faces and by their posture. If they are

Two young foxes play at fighting. They will learn which of them is the stronger.

A fox cub knows just how to get its mother's attention.

pleased to see each other they wag their tails. If ready for a fight they snarl and arch their backs. A fox wishing to **appease** another fox will lower its body close to the ground.

Smell is another way foxes get in touch. They mark out their ranges by spraying urine and leaving their droppings in special places such as tree stumps, boulders and clumps of grass. Other foxes passing by can tell that the area is the home of another fox. Foxes also mark the places they have hidden food.

Foxes smell each other when they meet.

5
Foxes and People

In the country foxes are generally considered to be pests. This one has been killed by a gamekeeper.

Foxes and Rabies

Rabies is a deadly disease that infects people, their farm animals (such as cattle and sheep) and wild animals, like foxes. This disease is caused by a tiny organism called a **virus**. Some of the red foxes in Europe, North and South America and Asia have rabies. If infected foxes bite another animal they pass on the virus in their **saliva**.

People can get rabies from infected dogs and cats. The disease makes some dogs and cats furious and they bite anyone who comes near them. If a person catches rabies they may die unless given a **vaccine** soon after being bitten. Vaccines help us fight off infectious diseases like rabies. Doctors usually give us vaccines by injections. In western countries dogs and cats are also given injections to stop them getting rabies. So people in these countries do not catch rabies from their pets.

Britain, Australia and New Zealand are free of rabies so extra care is taken to stop people bringing infected animals into these countries. People who want to bring their pets from countries where rabies is present must put them into **quarantine**. This means they are kept in isolation for four to six months. If they are infected with rabies the symptoms will appear during this time and the animal will have to be destroyed.

In some countries where foxes have rabies their numbers are kept down to try to stop the disease spreading. It is difficult to destroy all the foxes in an area. Those that are killed may be replaced by foxes from other areas. Scientists are now giving foxes vaccines to see if this helps to wipe out rabies. They bury food with the rabies vaccine hidden inside for the foxes to eat.

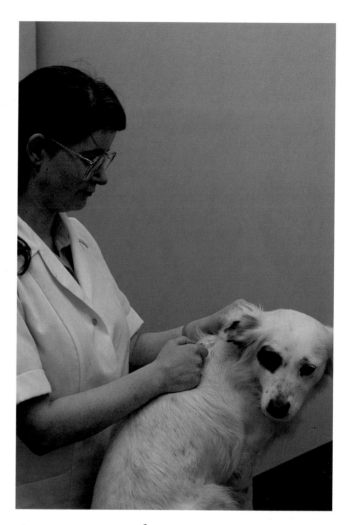

A vet gives a pet dog an injection. Domestic animals can be protected from catching rabies by vaccination.

Foxes as Pests

Foxes that live near people can be pests. Some foxes that live on farmland annoy farmers because they steal their chickens. Sometimes a fox

Foxes can be a nuisance in towns if they tear open garbage bags in search of tasty scraps.

will get into a hen house and kill many birds even though it could not eat them all. Foxes may be blamed for killing other farm animals like lambs. But foxes are probably just **scavengers** eating lambs that have already died because they were ill.

Most people who live in cities like to see foxes in their gardens and parks. But foxes can be unpopular if they eat small pets such as rabbits kept in the garden. They can be troublesome if they dig holes in the garden and leave smelly messages for other foxes. Cubs can be particularly naughty, scattering food about and squashing flowers.

Foxes are often blamed for the damage done by other animals. In towns, cats and dogs will be just as likely to raid your dustbin as foxes. In the countryside stray dogs may kill the farmer's lambs. Foxes do kill gamebirds and eat their eggs but cats are often more of a problem to gamekeepers than foxes.

Foxes like gardens where there are plenty of bushes to hide amongst.

Enemies of Foxes

Adult foxes are rarely eaten by other animals. In some places foxes are attacked by wolves. If cubs stray from the den they may be eaten by other animals. Big birds like eagles swoop down and carry off cubs to eat.

The main enemies of foxes are people and their dogs. People have

Below *Hunting foxes with horses and hounds is traditional, but many people feel it is cruel and would like it banned.*

Above *People hunt foxes with dogs. A terrier is sniffing at the entrance to a den.*

hunted the red fox for hundreds of years. In Britain hunting foxes on horseback with a pack of hounds is a traditional sport. Today some people think this is cruel, so hunting has stopped in some places. People also hunt foxes on foot with dogs trained to kill them. In some countries foxes are hunted with guns.

Foxes are not always killed for sport. People kill foxes where they are pests and have been killing chickens, ducks and gamebirds. Fox numbers are also controlled in places where they carry rabies. In towns and cities many foxes are run over accidentally by cars and killed.

Foxes are often killed for their beautiful fur. People make fur coats from the skin of foxes. These skins are called **pelts**. Foxes are trapped in the wild or bred on special farms. The fur from coloured varieties of some kinds of foxes is highly valued, like silver fox fur that comes from a type of red fox and blue fox fur that comes from the dark variety of the Arctic fox. Fox fur coats are a luxury, although not everyone wants to wear them. Some people feel fox furs suit foxes better than people.

A fox fur like this was once the height of fashion.

Fox Tales

We often think foxes are clever animals, possibly because they seem to outwit people when they escape from huntsmen or break into the hen house. We use the expression 'as cunning as a fox' to describe a clever person. Foxes do look rather crafty so it is easy to believe that they are up to no good.

There are many stories about foxes. Some have been passed on from one

The fox's crafty look has given it a reputation as a cunning animal.

generation to the next for centuries. So long, in fact, that no one is quite certain who told them in the beginning.

The popular animal stories, Aesop's Fables, are thought to have been told by a slave who lived about 600 BC in ancient Greece. In these stories foxes and other animals act rather like people and show us just how silly we can be, like the story of 'The fox and the crow'. The crow sitting high up in the branches of a tree has a large piece of cheese in its beak that the fox down on the ground would like to eat. The fox tricks the crow. He makes her sing, so she opens her beak and drops the cheese.

Foxes do not always get their own way in stories. In the Uncle Remus stories Brer Rabbit is the one who outwits poor old Brer Fox. In real life foxes are more successful at catching rabbits.

6
Learning More About Foxes

The entrance to a fox's den can be hard to see. Here is one dug into a grassy bank, beneath a bush.

Finding Foxes

The fox you are most likely to see is a red fox. They can be hard to find. If you have not actually seen a fox in your area, here are some clues which may help you to find them. Look out for their foot prints in mud or snow. These are called tracks. Fox prints are similar to those made by small dogs but are more oval in shape. You may also see the droppings left by foxes. These are drawn out into a point at one end. Reddish fur caught on thorny bushes or on the bottom strand of barbed wire fences is another clue that foxes are about.

If you are lucky you may find a fox's den. This could be a burrow in a wood or a hole under a garden shed. There should be a strong smell if foxes are living there. In spring you may find bones and feathers scattered around the entrance to the den. These are the

Right *A fox has a drink of melted snow.*

remains of the cubs' meal.

People sometimes discover they have foxes living nearby because they hear them barking. You may be able to find a fox by watching how birds behave. If a fox is about they will be alarmed and some, like crows and ravens, will swoop down and mob a fox to drive it away.

Below *These are some of the signs that a fox is about – footprints in the snow, droppings, or red hair caught on barbed wire.*

Watching Foxes

Foxes are usually secretive. City foxes tend to be bolder and less frightened of people than country foxes. So if you are in a city where foxes live you may be able to see them. Dawn and dusk are good times to see foxes. Although you can see them in the day –

The best time to see a fox in the country is dawn or dusk.

sometimes sunning themselves or searching for food, particularly when they have cubs. Some people put out food in their gardens for foxes to eat. Once foxes get used to the garden they are often regular visitors.

When watching foxes you must be very quiet and keep still. Otherwise they will be scared and run away. You must be very careful if you find a den with cubs, because if you frighten the mother she will move the cubs somewhere else. Often it is best to watch foxes from a place where they cannot see you. People who watch wildlife usually use something to hide behind, such as a canvas tent. This is called a **hide**.

You may get a good view of a fox family if you hide behind a bush and keep very still and quiet.

Finding Out More

If you would like to find out more about foxes, you could read the following books:

L.Bueler, *Wild Dogs of the World* (Constable, 1974).

D. Macdonald (editor), *The Encyclopaedia of Mammals: 1* (George Allen & Unwin, 1983).

S. Harris, *Urban Foxes* (Whittet, 1986).

J.D. Henry, *Red Fox* (Smithsonian Institution Press, 1986).

J. Pope, *The Fox* (Hamish Hamilton, 1984).

K. Taylor, *Foxes* (A & C Black, 1983).

Schnieper, *On The Trail of the Fox* (Dent, 1986).

Other Sources:

Royal Society for Nature Conservation
The Green
Nettleham
Lincoln LN2 2NR

The World Wildlife Fund
Panda House
12–13 Ockford Road
Goldalming
Surrey

London Zoo
Regents Park
London NW1 4RY

You can tell by the blood on his muzzle that this young fox has just eaten.

Glossary

Appease To behave in a friendly way towards a fox that is being threatening so that it will not attack.

Camouflage Colour and pattern of an animal that blends in with its surroundings. Camouflage helps an animal stay hidden from its enemies and from other animals it is trying to catch.

Carnivores Meat-eating animals.

Den A fox's home.

Hide A structure used by people to keep them hidden while they watch wild animals.

Home range The area in which an animal lives and finds food.

Litter A group of baby animals, born at the same time, from the same mother.

Mate The way in which male and female animals join together to produce young.

Moulting Shedding fur.

Muzzle The jaws and nose of the fox.

Nocturnal Active at night.

Northern hemisphere The half of the world north of the equator.

Pelt The skin taken from an animal.

Pregnant When an animal has a baby growing inside it.

Quarantine When an animal is kept in isolation to prevent a disease from entering a country.

Saliva Mouth juices that make food easier to swallow.

Scavenger An animal that eats animals that have already died or been killed by another animal. This includes scraps of meat and bones found in garbage.

Tundra A cold treeless region where the deeper part of the soil is always frozen.

Vaccine A substance that prepares the body to fight against a disease. Most vaccines are given to us by injections.

Virus A minute organism that can only be seen with a very powerful microscope. It lives inside the cells of other organisms. Viruses often cause diseases like rabies and the common cold.

Index

Picture Acknowledgements

All photographs from Oxford Scientific
Films by the following photographers:
M. Austerman (Animals Animals) 14;
Anthony Bannister 12, 21 (right); G.I.
Bernard 8, 9, 20, 23, 24, 26, 34, 42; Mike
Birkhead 19; David Cayless *cover*, 11; M.J.
Coe 15; Richard Davies 38; Terry Heathcote
41; Leonard Lee Rue III (Animals Animals)
17, 18; Tony Martin 16; Seiichi Meguro
frontispiece, 22, 25, 27, 28, 29 (left and
right), 36, 39, 40; Carsten R. Olesen/Foci 13
(left); Stan Osolinski 10; Press-tige Pictures
13 (right); Robin Redfern 21 (left), 32; Anna
Walsh 31, 35; M. Wilding 33; S.R.J. Woodell
30; The photograph on page 34 is from
Bruce Coleman. Illustrations on pages 37
and 39 are by Jackie Harland.